A COMMITMENT TO EXCELLENCE

Aerial view, Ponce de Leon Hall

The Rotunda of Ponce de Leon Hall — murals by George W. Maynard

A view of the courtyard, Ponce de Leon Hall

FLAGLER COLLEGE

*Twenty Five
Years of
Progress and Achievement*

Photographed by Tommy L. Thompson

HARMONY HOUSE
PUBLISHERS-LOUISVILLE

Editors: William Strode and William Butler
Library of Congress Catalog Number: 93-77064
ISBN 1-56469-003-2
Printed in Canada
First Edition printed Spring, 1994
by Harmony House Publishers,
P.O. Box 90, Prospect, Kentucky 40059
(502) 228-2010 / 228-4446

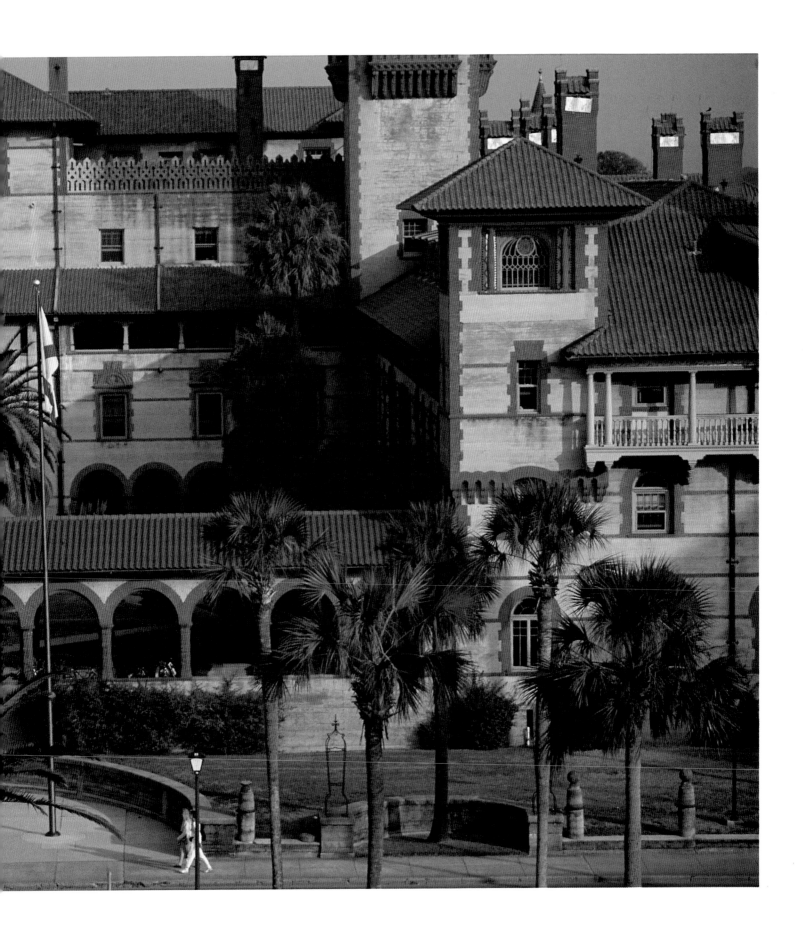

An aerial view of St. Augustine and Anastasia Island

INTRODUCTION

Following the footprints of many of America's most prestigious colleges and universities, Flagler College experienced difficult beginnings. Along with many of the nation's small independent colleges, Flagler faced an enormous challenge at its beginnings as a women's college in 1968. Inflation was rampant. Public universities were expanding rapidly. Authorities were projecting significant declines in the number of high school graduates who would seek higher education. Additionally, all of higher education had passed through a well-documented period of turbulence and discord.

In 1971, Flagler College, still in its infancy, underwent a comprehensive reorganization. Dr. William L. Proctor was named president of the College. That same year the College became coeducational. Reorganization represented a momentous undertaking for the administration of the College, but it also held great promise. The situation demanded careful planning, innovative approaches, and, most importantly, efficient management. It meant that new goals would be established and new procedures for success would be initiated.

With the support of the Board of Trustees, the administration began to formulate an important strategy for the College. The mission of Flagler College was clarified and four fundamental principles were identified. These principles would guide the institution's future:

• Flagler College would be concerned primarily with the instruction and advisement of undergraduate students;

• The College would provide an academic program composed of carefully selected, but limited, major programs of study;

• Student life would be guided by traditional standards;

• All plans and activities would be geared to the most efficient use of the College's resources.

A crucial factor in the College's early development was enrollment. At the time of reorganization, Flagler was an unknown college, and potential students and parents were hesitant to consider Flagler as a college choice. The dedication, persistence, and expertise of the admissions staff helped the College overcome its visibility problem during its formative years. Today, the Office of Admissions plays an important role in the College's continued success.

Since the College's founding in 1968, its growth and development have been determined largely by seven major events: the reorganization of the College in 1971; the achievement of regional accreditation in 1973; the establishment of the endowment fund in 1978; the renovation of Kenan Hall in 1982; the construction of Lewis House in 1987; the renovation and restoration of Wiley Hall in 1988; and the construction of the Flagler College Auditorium in 1990. Each of these events made possible the attainment of higher standards of quality, and each contributed to the stability and growth of the College.

The reorganization of 1971 brought new leadership to the College and laid the foundation for future development. Accreditation meant respectability and credibility for the College, and it provided assurance to prospective students and their parents that Flagler met prescribed standards of educational quality. The establishment of an endowment signified stability, and it engendered a sense of confidence among the College constituents. Both accreditation and endowment were vital to the early progress of the institution.

The renovation of Kenan Hall, through the support and generosity of the William R. Kenan, Jr. Charitable Trust and the Flagler Foundation, remedied a most crucial need for additional classrooms, laboratories, and faculty offices. It also provided for the expansion of the College library. The construction of Lewis House, through the generous support of Mr. Lawrence Lewis, Jr., the Flagler Foundation, and the William R. Kenan, Jr. Charitable Trust, provided a 180-bed men's residence hall. Lewis House enabled the College to strengthen its student recruitment program for men and to enhance the residential nature of the student body. The renovation of Wiley Hall, made possible through the support and generosity of Mrs. Mary L. F. Wiley, provided attractive offices for Admissions, Registrar, Financial Aid, Career Planning, and faculty, all of which, today, play a key role in the recruitment and retention of students. The construction of the Auditorium has enabled the College to enhance its educational programs and to reach out to the community through expanded cultural offerings.

The magnificent Hotel Ponce de Leon still stands as the centerpiece of the distinctive Flagler campus. Twenty-five years ago, Lawrence Lewis, Jr., at the time President of Flagler Systems, initiated a plan to convert the famous Hotel Ponce de Leon into a memorial for Henry Morrison Flagler. Soon afterward, Mr. Lewis was also responsible for the former hotel becoming the site of Flagler College, and he played a leadership role in the establishment of the College. His leadership and generous support carried the institution through the difficult period of reorganization. Flagler College is indebted to the vision, ingenuity, and benevolence of Mr. Lewis, his family, and the Kenan and Wiley families.

Ponce de Leon Hall was not only the first facility but also the legacy that launched Flagler College. In the years since the College's reorganization, restorations, renovations, and new construction have remarkably extended the campus. Today, the Flagler campus consists of twelve buildings, eight of which are historic structures.

The College continues to demonstrate a commitment to excellence, as evidenced by its prominent reputation among the state's colleges and universities. Since the reorganization in 1971, enrollment has increased from 223 students to more than 1,300 students in the fall of 1993. The number of students applying for admission has also increased dramatically. For the fall of 1993, the College received four applications for every space in the incoming class of new students. The average SAT score of entering freshmen was 89 points above the national average for college-bound seniors. With this growth and progress, the College has retained the personal contact essential to its mission. Small classes and close interaction among faculty, staff, and students prevails. The faculty remains dedicated to providing the highest quality of instruction.

More than 22 years ago, Dr. William L. Proctor faced the enormous challenge of establishing and defining the character of the College. He succeeded in meeting that challenge, and has since provided the dedicated and caring leadership needed to provide Flagler with a promising future.

LIFE'S·DVLL·ROVND,
·MAY·HAVE·BEEN,
STILL·HAS·FOVND·
ME·AT·AN·INN·✴

The marble stairway leading to the Dining Hall

A view of Ponce de Leon Hall from the grounds of the City Building and Lightner Museum, the former Alcazar Hotel, also built by Henry M. Flagler

An aerial view of Ponce de Leon Hall.

Arches, terra cotta work, and a grand fountain all add to the architectural beauty of Ponce de Leon Hall.

The distinctive skyline of St. Augustine

Historic Markland House

A view of the College Auditorium, constructed in 1990.

Memorial Presbyterian Church was built by Henry M. Flagler in memory of his daughter, Jennie Louise Benedict.

Grace Methodist Church, also built by Henry M. Flagler

Relaxing on the west lawn near Kenan Hall.

Ponce de Leon Hall, built in 1887, is listed in the National Register of Historic Places.

IN THE BEGINNING... THE HOTEL

Henry Morrison Flagler

The origins of the Hotel Ponce de Leon date back to the winter of 1885, when Henry M. Flagler, the very wealthy New York oil man, brought his second wife, Alice Shourds Flagler, to St. Augustine for the winter. The elite of northern society, it seems, had begun discovering the city as a resort and spa location.

The Flaglers took rooms at a hotel in the city, but the accommodations at the time were not up to Mr. Flagler's standards. This prompted him to begin thinking of building hotels in St. Augustine. He commented at the time that he wanted to make the city the "Newport of the South." Good to his word, shortly before the "Gay '90s," Mr. Flagler became one of the foremost tourist promoters in Florida.

In planning the construction of the Hotel Ponce de Leon, Mr. Flagler went to the New York firm of McKim, Meade and White, which at the time was one of the leading architectural firms in the nation. He proceeded to hire two young architects, John M. Carrere and Thomas Hastings. Both men had studied at the Ecole de Beaux-Arts in Paris and were trained in the style of French Renaissance. Mr. Flagler had a long-standing friendship with Hastings' father, and many believed this was much of the reason why he hired the two men. The construction firm of McGuire and McDonald was employed to build the hotel.

The site for the hotel was prepared by dumping tons of sand into the marshes located on the property. The foundations were poured of a very strong concrete mixture of one part sand, two parts coquina shell gravel and one part cement. The only iron reinforcement in the building was in the spans over arches, the longest being 22 feet. When completed in May 1887, the Hotel Ponce de Leon was the first major structure in the United States constructed principally of poured concrete.

For the interior design of the hotel, Mr. Flagler employed Louis Comfort Tiffany of New York. Tiffany at the time had reorganized his company to specialize in glass for architects and builders. Along with creating the ornate interior look of the hotel, the windows Tiffany designed had an important impact on making his name synonymous with excellence in glass.

The rotunda and dining hall of the Ponce de Leon were decorated with murals by George W. Maynard. The ceiling of the grand parlor (now the Flagler Room) was covered with angelic canvasses by Virgilio Tojetti. The interior was accentuated by using carved wood, imported marbles, oriental carpets, ornate furniture, exquisite vases, and beautiful paintings.

Utilities for the hotel were provided by the most modern and creative devices of the time. Four direct current dynamos were located in the boiler plant to generate electricity for lighting. Water for the Ponce de Leon was pumped from artesian wells. Because the water contained sulphur, it was piped through several fountains on the hotel grounds to aerate it before it was pumped into the twin towers of the hotel.

During its first five years of operation the Ponce de Leon was reputedly the most exclusive winter resort in the United States. President Grover Cleveland visited the hotel during its second month of operation. Four other presidents visited the hotel, along with various other celebrities and dignitaries.

With the opening and successful operation of the Ponce de Leon and two other hotels in St. Augustine, Flagler turned his full attention, and $60 million of his fortune, to the development of Florida's East Coast.

Flagler stretched his "Florida East Coast Railway" southward to Key West, built eleven luxury resort hotels, and founded what is now the Florida Power and Light Company. At one time Flagler owned more than 3.5 million acres of Florida real estate.

The legacies of Henry Flagler — the buildings and institutions he created— remain in the city of St. Augustine, where Flagler College stands with a beauty that has not faded with the years.

The Hotel Ponce de Leon under construction in 1886

The Ponce de Leon was the center of social activities during the hotel's winter season.

The courtyard of the Ponce de Leon was the "meeting place" for many of the hotel's guests.

Mary Lily Kenan Flagler and Henry Morrison Flagler

Driveway and parking area of the former hotel

Lawrence Lewis, Jr.

LAWRENCE LEWIS, JR.

Mr. Lawrence Lewis, Jr., receiving the La Florida Award, the City of St. Augustine's highest honor.

Lawrence Lewis, Jr., was born in Wilmington, North Carolina on July 6, 1918. In that same year, he moved with his family to St. Augustine to occupy Kirkside, the Flagler home, which his mother, Louise Wise Lewis, had recently inherited. Mrs. Lewis was the niece of Henry and Mary Flagler. Kirkside was located next to the Memorial Presbyterian Church. Mr. Lewis made his home in St. Augustine until 1938.

Mr. Lewis attended Woodberry Forest School and the University of Virginia, where he was a member of Phi Kappa Sigma and ODK. He enlisted in the Armored Force after the attack on Pearl Harbor, and served in a tank destroyer battalion in the Italian Campaign.

Mr. Lewis has had various business interests in Virginia, North Carolina, Florida, and the Bahamas, and he was President and Chief Executive Officer of Flagler System, Inc., until he retired in 1975.

Not since Henry Morrison Flagler descended on St. Augustine has one man so affected the nation's oldest city. In addition to his many civic contributions, Mr. Lewis has been a driving force behind the development of Flagler College, for it was he who saved Flagler's magnificent Hotel Ponce de Leon and engineered its re-birth as Flagler College.

Mr. Lewis served as Chairman of the Board of Trustees of Flagler College for more than 20 years, guiding the College through a very difficult time of reorganization in 1971. Since then, he has directed millions of dollars through foundation, family, and personal funds into new construction, restoration projects, endowment, and various other programs to ensure the success of Flagler College.

In the City of St. Augustine, Mr. Lewis has aided in the restoration of numerous Spanish Colonial structures; he has also funded studies of the colonial period. In cooperation with the College, he provides the necessary funds to support the work of the Center for Historic Research at Flagler College. He also has produced two films depicting the city's history and origins.

As Flagler College celebrates its twenty-fifth year, the recognition of its progress and continued success must, in large measure, be attributed to Henry M. Flagler's heir, Mr. Lawrence Lewis, Jr. "There would not be a Flagler College today without the vision, dedication, leadership, and generosity that Lawrence Lewis has bestowed upon this institution," said Dr. William L. Proctor, president of the College.

THE BIRTH OF THE COLLEGE

The Hotel Ponce de Leon went through many changes during the early and mid-1900s — busy, prosperous seasons and slow seasons when the hotel was less than one-fourth occupied.

The hotel was used from 1942 to 1945 for a U. S. Coast Guard training center. Other resort hotels in Florida were used by the military during this time also.

The end of the war began a return to prosperity for St. Augustine and the Ponce de Leon. Large crowds visited northern Florida during the late 1940s; however, beginning the decade of the '50s, each year saw fewer and fewer guests return to the Ponce de Leon. State government surveys identified the reasons why: only eight of every 100 Florida tourists preferred the northeast part of the state; only 13 of every 100 tourists needed accommodations in hotels. Most of the visitors of the time traveled in cars, and many came in the summer months when the hotel was closed.

In the early 1960s, the square in downtown St. Augustine was bordered by old hotels — the Ponce de Leon, the Alcazar, and the Cordova. Many townspeople thought that the area had become "a blighted eyesore." The Cordova building was no longer a hotel, empty except for shops on its street level. The Alcazar had been closed from 1932 until 1947, when it was purchased by O.C. Lightner for use as a museum. Lightner used only a few of the rooms and did little to maintain the remainder of the building. The Ponce de Leon, still a hotel, was the only one of the buildings that was maintained to any degree.

Other American cities had decided to solve problems such as this by razing buildings. St. Augustine's civic leaders responded with solutions to preserve and make use of these historic buildings. In 1961, the St. Johns County Commission purchased the Cordova Hotel from the Florida East Coast Hotel Company, and in 1968 the building reopened as the County Courthouse after undergoing a complete renovation. Two months before the completion of the Cordova, the St. Augustine City Commission elected to remodel the Alcazar as a city building. The work on the Alcazar was completed in 1972.

The fate of the Hotel Ponce de Leon itself was announced on January 18, 1967, when Flagler Systems' President Lawrence Lewis, Jr., announced to community leaders and the press that the famed hotel had been sold to a group of educators headed by Dr. F. Roy Carlson, president of Mount Ida Junior College, to house a new four-year private liberal arts college for women. The college was to be named Flagler College. Mr. Lewis stressed in his announcement that "exhaustive surveys by experts in hotel operation, as well as our own experience, proved that it was absolutely unfeasible to continue to operate this magnificent structure as a hotel."

Mr. Lewis made the announcement during a luncheon at which he introduced Dr. Carlson. The purchase price of the building was quoted at $1,500,000. The College would become Florida's first private, nondenominational, liberal arts college for women. During the luncheon, it was announced that the College would open for its first freshman class in the fall of 1968.

On September 24, 1968, Flagler College officially opened its doors. During an opening convocation held at Memorial Presbyterian Church, Dr. Carlson told the 180 members of the College's first freshman class, "We are here to help you become the finest people you are capable of becoming." Other activities for that first orientation week included a barbecue in the Arrivas House hosted by members of the Retail Merchants Division of the Chamber of Commerce, student assemblies, a student and faculty tea hosted by the Altrusa Club, two student talent nights, and a Sunday afternoon boat ride, courtesy of Captain Francis Usina.

Mr. Harry R. Gonzalez,
Flagler College Trustee

Mr. John D. Bailey, Sr.,
Flagler College Trustee

Dr. William J. McClure,
Flagler College Trustee

The Honorable Howell W.
Melton, Flagler College
Trustee

Lawrence Lewis, Jr., Dr. William L. Proctor and Frank Harrold.

THE COLLEGE REBORN

On Tuesday evening, January 19, 1971, Lawrence Lewis, Jr., Chairman of the Board of Trustees of Flagler College, told a group of enthusiastic students, faculty and staff that "giving birth to a new college sometimes gives terrible pain, but, believe me, the baby is alive, thriving and healthy." His remarks were met with thunderous applause and cheers.

During the late part of 1970 and in early January 1971, there had been some anxious concern among the student body that the College might close at mid-year. Rumors of financial instability were rampant. Mr. Lewis told the group assembled that he would answer any questions and would, he hoped, put an end to speculation concerning the College's future.

At the assembly, Mr. Lewis confirmed that the College had faced a financial crisis, but he announced that Flagler System, Inc., was "forgiving a present mortgage" on the Ponce de Leon of over $1,000,000. "Your trustees now own this plant free and clear," Mr. Lewis told the jubilant crowd.

During the assembly, Mr. Lewis announced that he had accepted the resignations of Dr. F. Roy Carlson, Dr. Ed Carlson, and all members of the Carlson family from the Flagler College Board of Trustees. He advised students and faculty in attendance, that effective immediately, as Chairman of the Board of Trustees, he had reinstated Dr. Paul Everett. He also announced that Dean Robert F. Carberry had withdrawn his resignation. Mr. Lewis told the crowd that he could not speak for drama professor Tom Rahner. The crowd turned and looked at Rahner, who yelled out, "I'll stay!" amid the cheering of students.

Mr. Lewis told the crowd that the well-known and respected St. Augustine banker, Frank F. Harrold, had been named "temporary Chancellor of the College until the Board of Trustees has time to name a new president." Formation of a new Executive Committee of the Board of Trustees was also announced at the assembly. The committee would consist of Mr. Lewis, John D. Bailey, Sr., and Mr. Harrold.

In concluding his remarks to the crowd, Mr. Lewis asked for questions from the floor. There were none —

just more applause and cheering from the crowd. Mr. Lewis later stated in an interview that he was "impressed and moved by the tremendous spirit and dedication of our students and faculty." Concerning the crisis that had been averted, Mr. Lewis said, "We have won a battle, but not the war. He added that " we will continue to look for help and support from the community, the state, and other sections of the nation."

On May 7, 1971, Mr. Lewis announced the appointment of Dr. William L. Proctor as President of Flagler College, effective immediately. Dr. Proctor was at the time Dean of Men and Assistant to the Vice President for Student Affairs at Florida Technological University, now the University of Central Florida, in Orlando. In announcing Dr. Proctor's appointment, Mr. Lewis stated that "the charm of this ancient city and the favorable prospects for the outstanding success of Flagler College were forcefully demonstrated by the fact that the announcement of the vacancy in the presidency of the College resulted in the receipt of some 350 applications for the post."

In introducing Dr. Proctor to the students and faculty on that Friday afternoon, Mr. Lewis thanked them for their spirit, which had held the College together during the search for a new president. He praised the work of interim Chancellor Frank F. Harrold, for his untiring efforts and "tender loving care."

Dr. Proctor addressed those assembled, saying that, while he had enjoyed his work in the state university system, he welcomed the opportunity to come to Flagler College. He told the crowd that the interest and enthusiasm on the part of the Board of Trustees was a significant factor in his accepting the presidency of Flagler College. He outlined as his priorities for the College increasing enrollment, eliminating all operating indebtedness, making improvements to the physical plant, and attaining regional accreditation. He also called upon faculty, staff, and students to work toward shared goals and to resist the danger of fragmentation or division among students, faculty and administration, which was one of the problems facing colleges and universities of the day.

Dr. William L. Proctor awards student Carl Williams the Presidential Award of Excellence.

DR. WILLIAM LEE PROCTOR

It is not accidental that the beginning of Flagler's fast rise to prominence coincided with the appointment of Dr. William L. Proctor as president. Dr. Proctor's blend of enthusiasm, discipline, and prudent business practices have been the driving force behind the remarkable progress of Flagler College.

The decision in 1971— to redefine and broaden Flagler's role from a small women's college to a coeducational institution of now more than 1,300 students— required a leader with the vision and the ability to make that vision a reality. Dr. Proctor was selected from approximately 350 candidates for the position.

His first years as the chief executive and chief academic officer were devoted to achieving academic credibility through regional accreditation and to developing sound financial practices. Early goals included the development of the curriculum and student activities program, and the recruitment of a strong faculty whose qualifications and aspirations were consonant with the redefined mission of the College. Validation of these goals came quickly — the college attained its initial accreditation in 1973, and established its endowment fund in 1978 through several major gifts.

Throughout his 22-year tenure as president, Dr. Proctor has led Flagler in a continued pattern of controlled growth. The College has evolved tremendously from the small, fledgling institution that it was at the time of reorganization. The physical plant has been developed through renovation, restoration, and new construction with an approach to campus expansion that has, as its guiding principle, a policy of avoiding debt and deferred maintenance. The College, $1.2 million in debt in 1971, has operated with a balanced budget for the past two decades. Through careful fiscal management, the endowment fund has grown to more than $14 million. The policy of careful, controlled growth has served the College well in inflationary years, and it has enabled the College to plan its programs and expenditures in an orderly fashion. The new library, scheduled for completion in 1995, follows this pattern.

Under Dr. Proctor's leadership, both enrollment and the quality of the academic program have increased significantly over the past two decades. A careful balance between growth and quality has been maintained to ensure that Flagler's professors and administrators are able to give each student the personal attention that is a distinctive feature of a small college.

A native of Atlanta, Georgia, Dr. Proctor has resided in Florida since 1944. He earned his bachelor's, master's, and doctorate degrees from Florida State University, and is the recipient of the "Distinguished Educator Award" from the College of Education at FSU. He is also a member of the "Athletic Hall of Fame," holds a second degree black belt in karate, and retains an active interest in golf and jogging.

In addition to Flagler duties, his professional involvements include the former chairmanship of the President's Council of the Independent Colleges and Universities of Florida, chairmanship of the Board of Trustees of the Florida School for the Deaf and the Blind, the presidency of the St. Augustine Foundation, and directorship of the St. Augustine/ St. Johns County Chamber of Commerce. He also serves on a number of state and national organizations: the American Association of Presidents of Independent Colleges and Universities, the Higher Education Panel of the American Council on Education, and the Board of Directors of the National Council of Agencies Serving the Blind.

Dean Robert Carberry cuts the cake at the celebration of the College's initial accreditation.

ACCREDITATION

The St. Augustine Record, May 1973
The president of Flagler College says he is "pleased with the report" handed in by an evaluation team from the Commission on Colleges of the Southern Association of Colleges and Schools and considers it to be "favorable and encouraging."

The visiting committee's report was presented Wednesday to Lawrence Lewis, Jr., chairman of the board of trustees of Flagler College, to Dr. William Proctor, president, and to other members of the administrative staff of the liberal arts college founded five years ago today.

Following submission of the visiting committee's report, Dr. Proctor and Dean Robert Carberry met with faculty, staff, and students to express appreciation for the "unity and cooperation displayed by all members of the College community."

Dr. Proctor said the report exceeded his expectations and "could not have been achieved without the combined efforts of trustees, faculty, staff, and students."

The committee's report will be submitted to the Commission on Colleges, and the Commission's recommendation is submitted to the College Delegate Assembly, which meets this December in Houston, Texas. Assuming a favorable vote by the College Delegate Assembly Flagler College could be fully accredited as of December 1973.

Dr. William L. Proctor addresses the faculty, staff, and students concerning the College's accreditation.

Kenan Hall

THE IMPORTANCE OF KENAN HALL

William R. Kenan, Jr.

Throughout his life, William R. Kenan, Jr., brother-in-law and business associate of Henry Morrison Flagler, believed in the value of a well-rounded education. In his will, Mr. Kenan designated a substantial part of his estate for the William R. Kenan, Jr. Charitable Trust. This trust has contributed millions of dollars to various institutions of higher learning in the United States.

What we now know as Kenan Hall, the College's primary academic facility, was formerly the quarters for hotel employees. The transformation of the building was made possible by a $3.5 million grant from the William R. Kenan, Jr. Charitable Trust, along with a $1.2 million grant from the Flagler Foundation. Kenan Hall was dedicated as a memorial to Mr. Kenan.

The grant from trustees of the Kenan Trust was made in the fall of 1980, and renovation of the building began in the spring of 1981. The building opened with the beginning of the fall semester in 1982.

The renovated Kenan Hall provided Flagler College with its first centralized academic building. It made possible the consolidation of over 80 percent of Flagler's academic facilities under one roof. "We started making plans for Kenan Hall as far back as 1969," said Robert A. Honiker, director of campus planning. "We started working on definitive plans in 1978, with actual construction beginning in 1981."

Because the condition of Kenan Hall had deteriorated badly over the years, the building's interior first had to be gutted. "We took out just about everything but the roof and exterior walls," Mr. Honiker said. He noted that it was "awesome" to enter the building at ground level and look up five stories and see the rafters.

The entire interior was rebuilt. Framing, joists, studs and decking all were replaced with steel. All new plumbing and wiring had to be installed. Changes were made to the electrical service, increasing it from 1,600 to 4,000 amps. An air conditioning and heating system was installed, along with elevators and other amenities.

The building now contains 12 classrooms, two seminar rooms, 32 faculty offices, the College's library, a 36-station natural science laboratory, five microcomputer laboratories, one modern foreign language laboratory, one writing laboratory, a learning disabilities clinic, and the kitchen servicing the adjacent student dining hall.

The statement of Executive Vice President William T. Abare, Jr., reflects the continuing importance of Kenan Hall to the growth and success of Flagler College: "The renovation and dedication of Kenan Hall is perhaps the most significant milestone event in the academic development of the College. It gave us real classrooms, faculty offices, laboratories, and space for an ever-expanding library collection. Kenan Hall truly reflected at that time, and continues to reflect, the ascending quality of the academic program at our College."

Dr. William L. Proctor addresses the audience gathered for the dedication of Kenan Hall.

Frank Kenan, John L. Gray, and Lawrence Lewis, Jr., at the dedication of Kenan Hall.

Members of the Kenan, Lewis, and Wiley families with Dr. William L. Proctor at the dedication of Kenan Hall.

The renovation of Kenan Hall

Lawrence Lewis, Jr. and William R. Kenan, Jr.

A night-time view of the exterior of the Dining Hall and Kenan Hall. The Dining Hall features the stained glass works of Louis Comfort Tiffany.

Various views of the Dining Hall featuring Maynard murals and Tiffany stained glass.

A view from one of the galleries of the Dining Hall. The main room is encircled with 100 gold lion heads with light bulbs in their mouths.

A picnic on the lawn of Ponce de Leon Hall.

Darwin White chats with student Nicole Andrews.

The Rotunda of Ponce de Leon Hall

Cherubs decorate much of the woodwork in Ponce de Leon Hall.

Ornate lighting and woodwork adorn Ponce de Leon Hall.

Tojetti murals and Tiffany chandeliers are part of the beautiful interior of the Flagler Room, formerly the Grand Parlor.

The focal point of the Flagler Room is the marble fireplace featuring one of the first electric clocks ever used in a public building.

The murals of George W. Maynard adorn the entryway, Rotunda and Dining Hall of Ponce de Leon Hall.

The interior of the Flagler College Auditorium

(Left to right) Mr. John D. Bailey, Sr., Mrs. Molly Wiley, and Dr. William L. Proctor at the dedication of Wiley Hall.

Mrs. Molly Wiley with Flagler student Russell Swanson, who presented her with a watercolor painting of Wiley Hall during the building dedication.

MOLLY LEWIS WILEY

Mr. Lawrence Lewis, Jr., and Mrs. Molly Wiley

Molly Lewis Wiley was born in St. Augustine, Florida on March 7, 1928. She and her brother Lawrence Lewis, Jr., lived with their parents in the Flagler home, Kirkside, which her mother inherited as the niece of Henry and Mary Flagler.

Mrs. Wiley made her home in St. Augustine until the death of her mother in 1938, at which time she moved to Richmond, Virginia to live with her father. She attended The Master's School at Dobbs Ferry, New York and St. Catherine's School in Richmond. Mrs. Wiley graduated from Kingsmith in Washington, D.C.

Since the inception of Flagler College, Mrs. Wiley has played an important and supportive role in the College's development. Wiley Hall, located at 6 Valencia Street, was the home in which she had lived during her childhood. Through her support, that building was completely reno-

vated, and it now houses the offices of Admissions, Career Planning, the Registrar, Financial Aid, and the faculty for the Business Administration Department.

Mrs. Wiley has generously contributed to other projects at the College, including the renovation of the Government House Theater, Molly's Place, and the Dining Hall.

Today, Mrs. Wiley continues her support of Flagler College. She provided the lead gift for the 1991-92 Flagler College Annual Fund. During the 1992-93 Annual Fund campaign, she matched each dollar given by alumni and friends of the College.

As the history of the College is retold through the years, no one will give a full account of Flagler without including one of the most significant and generous individuals in the development and progress of Flagler College, Mrs. Molly Lewis Wiley.

Members of the SGA Executive Board present a plaque to Mrs. Molly Wiley during the dedication of Molly's Place. Left to right are Will Verbits, Darla Mankel, Rick Bartl, Mrs. Molly Wiley, Delphine Jordan, and Glenn O'Brien.

Mrs. Clarissa Anderson Gibbs

Students on the front steps of Markland House.

CLARISSA ANDERSON GIBBS

Mrs. Clarissa Anderson Gibbs was born in St. Augustine on November 6, 1895. The daughter of Dr. Andrew Anderson, Jr., and Elizabeth Smethurst Anderson, Mrs. Gibbs grew up in the family home, Markland, which now is part of the Flagler College campus. Construction of the home began in 1839 by Dr. Andrew Anderson, Sr., and was completed after his death. The original house, however, was only half the size of the present structure. Extensive additions were made to the home about 1900, adding the west wing and replacing the square columns in front with massive, fluted, round columns.

It was at Markland that Mrs. Gibbs' father met frequently with Henry Morrison Flagler and encouraged him to begin his development of St. Augustine. This was Mr. Flagler's first step in turning Florida's east coast into the "American Riviera." Although a small child at the time, Mrs. Gibbs remembered those days and recounted many of Flagler's visits to Markland.

Mrs. Gibbs was a benefactor not only to Flagler College but also to the city of St. Augustine. In 1987 she received the Order of La Florida, the highest honor bestowed by the City of St. Augustine. This honor is presented to an individual who unselfishly devotes time and talent to the welfare and betterment of the city and its heritage. Mrs. Gibbs' interest in the city dates back to the early 1920s, when, as a young woman, she and her family presented the lions for the Bridge of Lions on behalf of her father. Dr. Anderson had commissioned the Italian artist, Romanelli of Florence, to reproduce the lions that adorn the Loggia di Lanzi in Florence.

Mrs. Gibbs' generosity to Flagler College included commissioning Flagler history professor Dr. Thomas Graham to write "The Awakening of St. Augustine: The Anderson Family and the Oldest City 1921-1924." She assisted Flagler College with the restoration of Markland House. In 1979, she was named a Champion of Higher Independent Education in Florida by the Independent Colleges and Universities of Florida.

Upon her death, January 21, 1990, Dr. William Proctor said of Mrs. Gibbs, "Certainly she was a very good friend of the College, but beyond that, she was a very delightful person, possessing a keen mind, a very quick wit, and a beneficent spirit. We'll simply miss her very much."

Mr. Lawrence Lewis, Jr., is shown with Lewis Scholars, from left: Nancy Deyo, Jamie Chatham, Ann Sagraves, Suzanne Novak, Michael Andres, Melanie Stecker and Todd Troyer.

Mr. Lawrence Lewis, Jr., and Dr. William L. Proctor address the audience during the dedication of Lewis House.

Lewis House, a men's residence hall for 180 students, is named for Mr. Lawrence Lewis, Jr.

Dining Hall ceiling murals prior to restoration

The Dining Hall of the Hotel Ponce de Leon

Dining Hall restoration work in progress

Workmen reinstall a Tiffany stained glass window in the Dining Hall. These particular windows were re-leaded and refurbished as part of the Dining Hall restoration project.

A view of the Dining Hall following completion of the restoration project

1992 NAIA National Doubles' Champions, Lindsey Ames, front, and Helena Dahlstrom, members of the Flagler College women's tennis team.

SPORTS

Tennis Coach Walter Shinn

SPEAKERS

General Alexander Haig Jr., former Secretary of State

Bettina Gregory, ABC News correspondent

Dr. Alan Greenspan, Federal Reserve Chairman

Jacques Cousteau, marine scientist and explorer

William Sessions, former Director, Federal Bureau of Investigation

Dr. Andrew Anderson, Jr.

CAMPUS

Markland House

Mrs. Mary L. F. Wiley

Wiley Hall

Mr. Lawrence Lewis, Jr.

Lewis House, men's residence hall

Chairmen of the Flagler College Board of Trustees: (from left to right): Mr. John D. Bailey, Sr., (1988-1992), Mr. Lawrence Lewis, Jr. (1969-1988) and the Honorable Frank D. Upchurch, Jr. (1992 to present).

Mr. William T. Abare, Jr., Executive Vice-President

Dr. William L. Proctor, President

85

Student activity at Kenan Hall

An architectural rendering of the proposed Flagler College Library

The General's House is the campus building that houses the Office of Business Services, the Office of Campus Planning, Gallaudet Regional Center, and the Center for Historic Research at Flagler College.

Because Flagler is a small college, the frequency and quality of faculty-student contacts are increased.
Dr. Dawn Wiles, Professor and Chairperson of the Foreign Languages Department, joined the faculty in 1972.

Flagler has assembled an outstanding faculty committed to teaching and advising
undergraduate students. Mr. Michael Sherman, Associate Professor and Chairman
of the Social Science Department, has been a member of the faculty since 1970.

Enzo Torcoletti, Professor of Art and
member of the faculty since 1971, is an
internationally recognized sculptor.

Flagler faculty are involved in their teaching field both on and off-campus. Dr. Andrew Dillon, Professor of English and a member of the faculty since 1972, enjoys writing poetry and lecturing before a variety of audiences.

Mr. Thomas Rahner, Associate Professor and Chairman of the Drama Department since 1968, holds the College mace.

Mr. Donald Martin, Associate Professor of Art since 1977, has received numerous awards for his art work.

Dr. J. Robin King, Associate Professor of Philosophy, talks with student Christopher Lange.

A main stage production of Agatha Christie's "The Hollow" in the Flagler College Auditorium.

90

Academic programs such as the nationally acclaimed Deaf Education program make Flagler a sought-after choice. Four applications for admission are received for every available space.

An aerial view of the Flagler College Tennis Center

Students walk through the courtyard of Ponce de Leon Hall on their way to class.

Helena Dahlstrom, of Bastad, Sweden, won NAIA National Women's Singles' Championships in 1991 and 1992.

Ponce de Leon Hall, Flagler College

MILESTONES

Dr. Paul Everett congratulates Beverly Copeland during the first commencement exercise. Dr. Copeland later was the College's Director of Development. Dr. William Proctor, center, and Dean Robert Carberry present Dinah Hopping with her diploma while Judy Nicholson looks on.

Mr. George Patthey, Superintendent of Plant and Grounds, has been with Flagler College since its inception.

The Visiting Committee appointed by the Commission on Colleges of the Southern Association of Colleges and Schools meets with members of the Board of Trustees and the administration in the spring of 1973.

1968-1969 *Flagler College founded as a four-year women's college.*
1970-1971 *Reorganized as a coeducational college.*
• Dr. William L. Proctor appointed President.
1971-1972 *Held first commencement exercise and graduated 35 students.*
1973-1974 *Received initial accreditation from the Commission on Colleges of the Southern Association of Colleges and Schools.*
• Awarded honorary degree to Mr. Lawrence Lewis, Jr., Chairman of the Board of Trustees, in recognition of his leadership and support through the reorganization of the College.

Page 96: *Dr. William L. Proctor and Mrs. Elizabeth Hudson at the 1993 Fall Convocation marking the College's 25th Anniversary. Mrs. Hudson has been with the College since its inception.*

Dr. George Green, Professor and Chairman of the Mathematics Department, joined the faculty in 1979.

Ceremony observing Ponce de Leon Hall being listed in the National Register of Historic Places.

Mr. Lawrence Lewis, Jr., raises high a pair of trophies at the dedication of the new Gymnasium.

1974-1975 *Renovation of Government House Theatre completed through the generosity of Mrs. James L. Wiley. • Ponce De Leon Hall listed in National Register of Historic Places.* **1976-1977** *Construction of Flagler College Gymnasium completed. • Men's tennis team won NAIA National Championships for team, singles, and doubles.*

Gordon Jones, a key member of the men's tennis team, which won Flagler's first NAIA national team championship in 1977. Jones also captured the singles' title and teamed with Jim Twigg to win the doubles' title.

Dr. William Proctor, ABC News correspondent Mr. Sam
Donaldson, and former U. S. Senator Edward Gurney
at the first Flagler Forum.

Dr. Anne Shreve, Professor and
former Chairperson of the
Education Department, honored
for her role in establishing the
Northeast Educational Consortium
which focuses on the deaf and
hearing impaired. Dr. Shreve
joined the faculty in 1974.
Also shown: Enzo Torcoletti.

Deaf education graduate Lou Greco, a 1992 finalist for Teacher
of the Year in Florida, teaches at the Florida School for the Deaf
and the Blind. He is also a part-time instructor at Flagler College.

Mr. Glenn Platt, Director of the Library
from 1975 to 1986.

1977-1978 *Established endowment fund with
$4 million gift from the Flagler Foundation.
• Flagler Field completed with funds provided by the President's Council. • Alumni
Association formed. • Deaf Education program certified by the Council on Education
of the Deaf. • Charter granted by Alpha Chi
National College Honor Scholarship Society.*
1979-1980 *Received $1.4 million gift from
the Jesse Kenan Wise Foundation for endowment. • First Flagler Forum held.*

Captian Henry F. "Hank" Lloyd served as Registrar for more than 20 years.

Kenan Hall was renovated for use as the College's main academic building.

The first Lewis Scholars, Todd Troyer and Suzanne Novak, make a presentation to College benefactor, Mr. Lawrence Lewis, Jr., at the dedication of Lewis House.

1980-1981 *Received $3.5 million grant from the William R. Kenan, Jr. Charitable Trust and $1.5 million grant from the Flagler Foundation for the renovation of Kenan Hall.*
1981-1982 *Renovation of Kenan Hall completed. Named for William R. Kenan, Jr., industrialist, philanthropist, brother-in-law and business associate of Henry M. Flagler. • Enrolled first Lewis Scholars.*

Dr. Constantine Santas, Professor and Chairman of the English Department, joined the faculty in 1971.

SAM Club sponsor, Mr. Louis Preysz, a member of the faculty since 1982, presents a trophy to club president, Greg Lund, for Flagler's SAM Chapter being selected as the outstanding new SAM Chapter in the nation.

Mr. Ernest Jones, College Recorder from 1968 to 1991.

Mrs. Dorothy Rooney served as Secretary for the Athletic Department from 1978 to 1993.

Dr. John Kistler, a member of the faculty in the Social Sciences Department from 1970 to 1993.

1982-1983 *Number of graduates from the College exceeds 1,000; actual total was 1,086.* • *Restoration of the first floor of Markland House completed.* **1983-1984** *Enrollment reaches 1,000 students.* • *Construction of Flagler College Tennis Center completed.* • *Flagler College chapter of the Society for Advancement of Management (SAM) selected as the most outstanding nationally.*

Mr. Ray Hull, Admissions staff member since 1980.

Col. Robert Honiker, Director of Campus Planning, joined Flagler in 1971.

Dr. Mattie Hart, Professor of Religion, joined the faculty in 1976.

Mr. Tom King, College Archivist, joined the College in 1983 as Director of Public Information. Secretary Joanne Moore joined a year later.

1984-1985 *Renovation of Molly's Place (Student Center and Student Lounge) completed; named for Mrs. James L. Wiley (Mary Lily Flagler Lewis). • Renovation of residence hall rooms in Ponce de Leon Hall completed. • Mr. Jacques Cousteau, marine explorer, addressed the College.*

Kristen Vatland and Laura Gervais in a renovated residence hall room of Ponce de Leon Hall.

Mr. Frank H. Kenan, left, accepts the first Flagler College Medallion from Mr. Lawrence Lewis, Jr., then Chairman of the Board of Trustees.

Mr. Peter Scott, coach of the men's tennis team from 1974-1991.

Mr. Jack Lakes, Vice President of Business and Finance, joined Flagler in 1974.

From left, Assistant Director of Gallaudet Regional Center Mr. Hugh Lewis; Dr. I. King Jordan, President of Gallaudet University; Dr. Roslyn Rozen, Dean of Continuing Education at Gallaudet; and Mr. Don Rhoten, Director of Southern Regional Center of Gallaudet University at the time that it was established on the campus of Flagler College.

Dr. Frances Farrell, Professor of Education, has been a member of the faculty since 1978.

1985-1986 *First Flagler College Medallion awarded to Mr. Frank H. Kenan, Chairman of the William R. Kenan, Jr. Charitable Trust. • Established offices on campus for the Southern Regional Center of Gallaudet University, the national university for the deaf. • Men's tennis team won second NAIA National Championship.*

Associate Professor and Chairman of the Art Department, Mr. Robert Hall, a member of the faculty since 1970, instructs former student Stacey Bissell, who is now a member of the Admissions staff.

Dr. Vincent Puma, Associate Professor of English, joined the faculty in 1973.

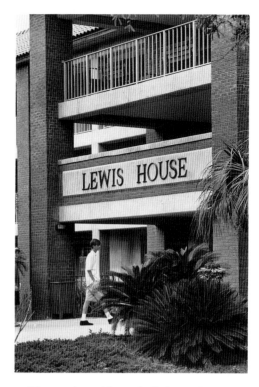

The men's residence hall, Lewis House, was built in 1986.

Mrs. Virginia DuBeau, College Nurse since 1983.

1986-1987 *Construction of Lewis House completed. The 180-bed residence hall was named for Mr. Lawrence Lewis, Jr. • Launched $2 million capital campaign for the restoration of the College Dining Hall. • Restoration of Twenty Valencia completed. • Established formal affiliation with the St. Augustine Foundation, Inc., to sponsor jointly the Center for Historic Research. • Awarded Flagler College Medallions to Dr. Todor Dobrovsky, Professor Emeritus, and to Dr. Paul E. Everett, Jr., Dean of the College (1968-1970). • Women's tennis team won its first NAIA National Championship.*

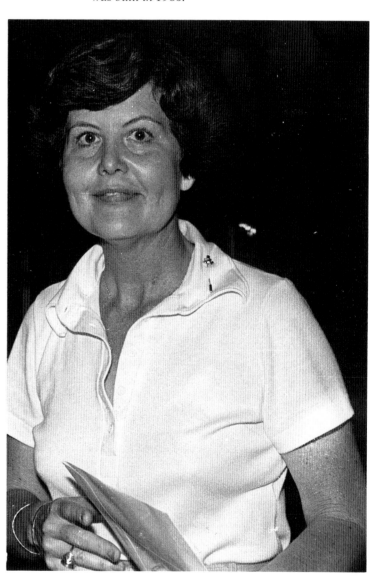

Ms. Pat Blair, College Counselor, has been a member of the Student Services staff since 1976.

In 1988, the number of Flagler College graduates exceeded 2,000.

The former Hotel Ponce de Leon, built in 1888 by Henry M. Flagler, now stands as the centerpiece of the Flagler College campus.

1987-1988 *Awarded Flagler College Medallion to Mr. Lawrence Lewis, Jr., Chairman of the Board of Trustees of Flagler College from 1968 to 1988.*
• Restoration of Nine Carrera completed. • Number of graduates exceeds 2,000 for the first time; actual total was 2,084. • Renovation of Grand Parlor completed. • Celebrated 100th Anniversary of the construction of the former Hotel Ponce de Leon.
• Women's tennis team won second consecutive NAIA National Championship.

Mr. Marc Sherrin, Assistant Professor of Mathematics, joined the College faculty in 1983.

Mrs. Pat Weddle, secretary to the Registrar, has served in several departments since joining Flagler in 1972.

Mr. Reuben Sitton, Director of Financial Aid, joined Flagler in 1978.

Dr. Steve Willard, Associate Professor of Psychology, joined the faculty in 1973.

Students eat in the restored Dining Hall.

1988-1989 *Restoration of building at Six Valencia completed; named Wiley Hall for Mrs. Molly Lewis Wiley. • Awarded $150,000 challenge grant from the Kresge Foundation for the capital campaign to restore the Dining Hall. • Renovation of the College Infirmary completed. • Received two awards from the Florida Trust for Historic Preservation: Twenty Valencia and the Grand Parlor, now the Flagler Room. • Women's tennis team won third consecutive NAIA National Championship.*

Mr. William T. Abare, Jr., Executive Vice President, joined the College administration as Dean of Admissions in 1971. He chats with Lewis Scholar Terri McGee.

*Flagler alumnus, Mr. Peter Meehan,
Director of Alumni Services and
former Director of Admissions, joined
the Admissions staff in 1976.*

*Dr. Peter Lardner, Professor and Chairman of the Natural
Science Department, has been a member of the faculty
since 1976.*

*Mrs. Barbara Carberry, Assistant Professor of Mathematics,
has taught at Flagler since 1980.*

*Markland House, constructed in 1839 and acquired by the
College in 1968, is now used extensively for social functions.*

1989-1990 *Received special category grant for
$414,712 from Bureau of Historic Preservation,
Department of State, for project to restore the Dining
Hall. Completed capital campaign to restore the
Dining Hall and exceeded the campaign goal of $2
million. • Combined value of endowment funds
exceeds $10 million for the first time. • Received
Award of Merit from Florida Trust for
Historic Preservation.*

107

Mr. Daniel Stewart, Dean of Student Services and former Athletic Director, instructor, and coach, joined the College in 1980.

Soccer Coach Bob Moullin joined the staff at Flagler College in 1982.

Ms. Phyllis Gibbs is now in her twenty-fourth year of teaching drama at Flagler College.

Darwin White, Registrar and former Dean of Students, joined the staff in 1975.

1990-1991 *Construction of Flagler College Auditorium completed. • Flagler's Society for Advancement of Management chapter won top honors in the case management competition at the International Meeting of SAM.*

The roof is lowered into place on the 65-foot tower of the Flagler College Auditorium.

Mr. William Kearney, Assistant Professor of Mathematics, joined the faculty in 1979.

Financial Aid Secretary Pat Mihovilich.

Dr. Thomas Graham, Professor of History and cross country coach, joined Flagler in 1973.

Dr. Jerry Noloboff, Professor of Psychology, joined the faculty in 1976.

1991-1992 *Initiated an Annual Fund to provide unrestricted support for the operating budget. • Flagler's SAM chapter won top honors in the case management competition at the International Meeting of the Society for Advancement of Management held at the University of Virginia in Charlottesville. It marked the first time in the 87-year history of SAM that a team has captured back-to-back first place finishes. • Enrollment reaches 1,224. • Women's tennis team wins NAIA National doubles' and singles' championships.*

Mrs. Anne Craft, Office of Academic Affairs, joined the staff in 1976.

Dr. Paul Crutchfield, Associate Professor and Chairman of the Education Department, joined the faculty in 1978.

The College plans to begin construction of the new library during the 1993-1994 academic year to replace the library in Kenan Hall.

1992-1993 *Received $5 million grant from the William R. Kenan, Jr. Charitable Trust for the construction of a new library.*
• Awarded Flagler College Medallion to Mr. Harry R. Gonzalez, a member of the Flagler College Board of Trustees from 1970-1993.

Mr. Peter Cramer, Director of Safety and Security, joined the College in 1983.

Ms. Helen Amato, Director of Career Planning, has been a member of the College staff since 1972.

110

Students Janis Sullivan, Jason Creasy and Dana Porter sport commemorative T-shirts.

Flagler College Radio, WFCF, goes on the air with student DJ's Christopher Carnley and Janeen Damiano, Communications majors.

Chairman of the President's Council, Sue Hale, presents a silver bowl to Judge Frank D. Upchurch, Jr., Chairman of the Board of Trustees, on the College's Silver Anniversary.

The Class of 1993-1994 processes to the Flagler College Auditorium.

1993-1994 *College celebrated its 25th Anniversary at the Fall Convocation. • St. Augustine Mayor Greg Baker proclaimed September 30, 1993 as Flagler College Day. • Flagler College's radio station, WFCF 88.5 FM, began broadcasting November 1, 1993. • Flagler's SAM chapter won first place for the third time in the case management competition at the international meeting.*